Languages Are Everywhere

Hi Reader,

My name is Nandi. I am a linguist. Linguists like to learn about how people communicate.

I love that people communicate in different ways. This is called *variation*.

Some people think variation is bad or wrong. Linguists, like me, know variation happens because everyone is unique! We think variation is exciting, interesting, and important!

You might communicate like the people in this book. You might not communicate like the people in this book. That is okay!

The way you communicate is awesome.
~ Dr. Nandi Sims

By Dr. Nandi Sims

T0020356

Rourke™

BEFORE AND DURING READING ACTIVITIES

Before Reading: *Building Background Knowledge and Vocabulary*

Building background knowledge can help children process new information and build upon what they already know. Before reading a book, it is important to tap into what children already know about the topic. This will help them develop their vocabulary and increase their reading comprehension.

Questions and Activities to Build Background Knowledge:

1. Look at the front cover of the book and read the title. What do you think this book will be about?

2. What do you already know about this topic?

3. Take a book walk and skim the pages. Look at the table of contents, photographs, captions, and bold words. Did these text features give you any information or predictions about what you will read in this book?

Vocabulary: *Vocabulary Is Key to Reading Comprehension*

Use the following directions to prompt a conversation about each word:

- Read the vocabulary words.
- What comes to mind when you see each word?
- What do you think each word means?

Vocabulary Words:
- bilingual
- deaf
- language
- symbol

During Reading: *Reading for Meaning and Understanding*

To achieve deep comprehension of a book, children are encouraged to use close reading strategies. During reading, it is important to have children stop and make connections. These connections result in deeper analysis and understanding of a book.

Close Reading a Text

During reading, have children stop and talk about the following:

- Any confusing parts
- Any unknown words
- Text to text, text to self, text to world connections
- The main idea in each chapter or heading

Encourage children to use context clues to determine the meaning of any unknown words. These strategies will help children learn to analyze the text more thoroughly as they read.

When you are finished reading this book, turn to the last page for an **After-Reading** activity.

Table of Contents

What Is Language?

People use language every day. But what is **language**?

Language is how people communicate with each other.

There are more than 6,000 different languages in the world!

We are using English. English is the most spoken language in the world.

Some people use more than one language. They are **bilingual**.

Nǐ hǎo means "Hello."

Liu's family is bilingual. They speak English and Chinese at home.

Two Types of Language

Hào chī!

English and Chinese are spoken. Liu uses her voice to communicate.

Language can also be signed. Rayan uses his hands and body to communicate.

Rayan and his mother are **deaf**. They sign ASL and know English. They are bilingual like Liu's family.

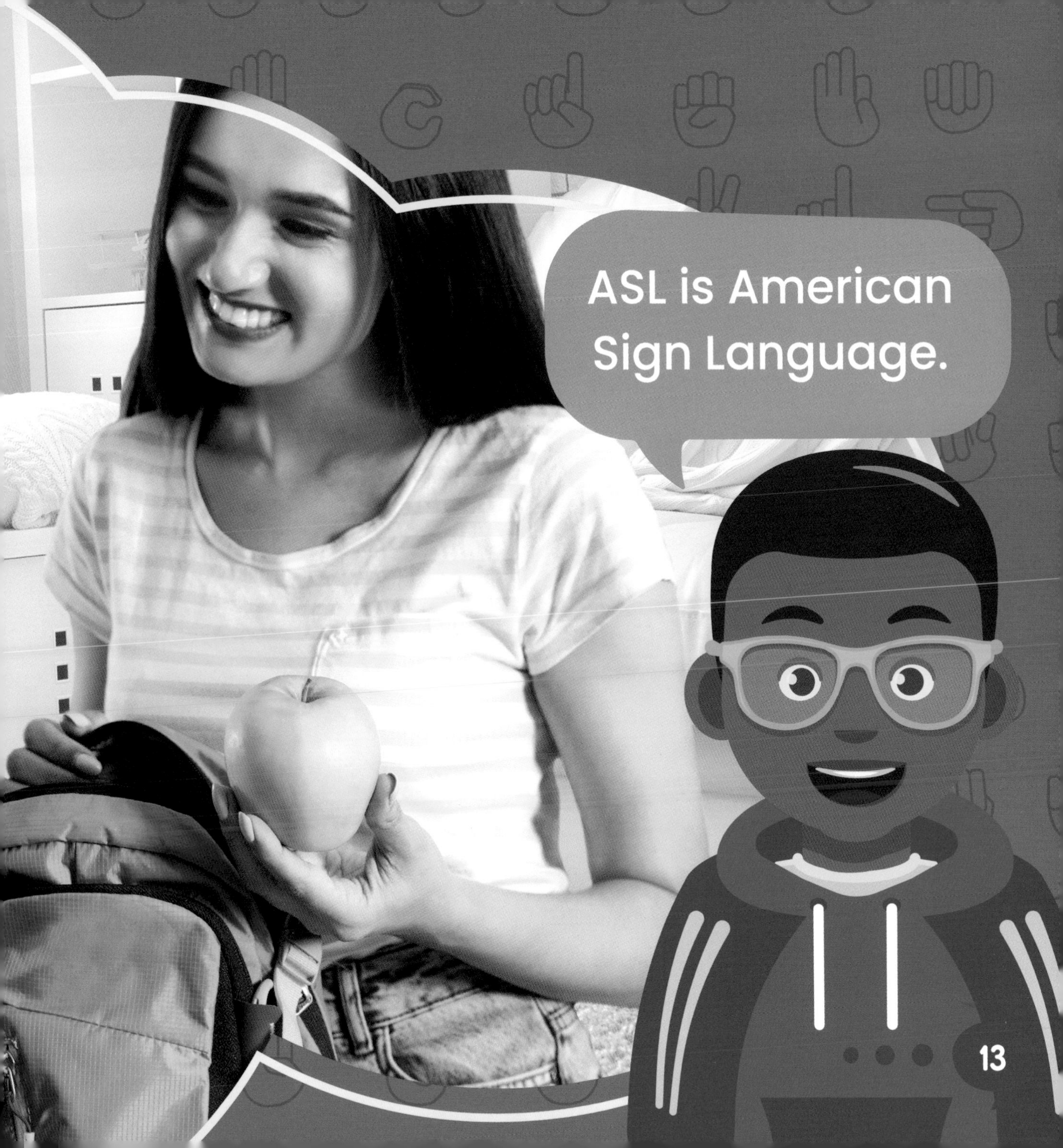

ASL is American Sign Language.

Liu wants to communicate with Rayan. She asked Rayan to teach her some words.

They are signing "play."

You can learn a new language. This is how you sign "hello" in ASL.

Reading and Writing

Most languages can be read and written. Liu and Rayan are learning to read and write.

"Hello" in ASL can be written with this **symbol**:

Letters are used to write English.

Hanzi are used to write Chinese.

Letters and hanzi are symbols.

There are many ways to communicate.

We love learning about languages!

Photo Glossary

bilingual (bye-LING-gwuhl): able to use two different languages

deaf (DEF): unable to hear

language (LANG-gwij): the use of words and sentences to communicate thoughts and feelings

symbol (SIM-buhl): a design or an object that stands for or represents something else

22

Activity: Watch and Learn

Supplies

paper
pencil
crayons/markers

Directions

1. Ask an adult to take you to a public park or a busy store.
2. Find a place to sit where you can observe how the people around you are communicating.
3. Write or draw your observations on your paper.

Do you understand what you see and hear? Are people using their voices, their bodies, or both? What did you learn about the languages people use in your community?

My observations:	Place: Stonybrook Park
	Time: 11:00am

Observations:

1. A man and a woman are talking to each other. They are using English. He moves his body a lot when he talks.

2. A little girl is talking to a baby. She is making silly noises.

Index

About the Author

Nandi Sims earned her PhD in Linguistics from The Ohio State University. She loves to research language variation in communities. When she is not researching, teaching, or writing, she is often dancing or walking one of her five dogs.

After-Reading Activity

Choose a place that is interesting to you. What language do the people speak? With a parent, go online and search how to say some everyday words and phrases in their language. Make a list of the words and phrases you learn.

Library of Congress PCN Data

Languages are Everywhere / Dr. Nandi Sims
(Words in My World)
ISBN 978-1-73165-274-4 (hard cover)(alk. paper)
ISBN 978-1-73165-244-7 (soft cover)
ISBN 978-1-73165-304-8 (e-book)
ISBN 978-1-73165-334-5 (e-pub)
Library of Congress Control Number: 2021952180

Rourke Educational Media
Printed in the United States of America
01-2412211937

www.rourkebooks.com

Edited by: Catherine Malaski
Cover design by: Tammy Ortner
Interior design by: Tammy Ortner
Photo Credits: Cover, p 2 © Dr. Nandi Sims, © Falcona, © fizkes, © antoniodiaz, © N.Savranska, © YamabikaY, p 4-5 © Studio Romantic, © Anna Kutukova p 6 © Ioannis Ioannou, © ksanaaa7 p 8-9 © Nattakorn_Maneerat, © Gerasimov Sergei p 10-11 © Serghei Starus, © Timmary, © Billion Photos, © M. Unal Ozmen, © Azindianlany p 12-13 © New Africa, © DesignPirate © Yuganov Konstantin, p 14-15 © New Africa, © Anastasiia_2305, p 16-17, © FatCamera, © ksanaaa7, p 18 © RobynCharnley, © Denissenko Oleg, © Becky Stares © Compack Background, p 19 © Adam Yee, © JingAiping, © Toa55, p 18-19 © HelenField, p 20-21 © Aysezgicmeli, p 21 © Pixel-Shot, p 22 ©Nattakorn_Maneerat, © Studio Romantic, © New Africa, © Toa55, p 24 © Dr. Nandi Sims